AF417359

SURFACE

Tash Lewington

BookLeaf Publishing

SURFACE © 2022 Tash Lewington

All rights reserved.

No part of this publication may be reproduced, stored in a retrieval system, or transmitted, in any form or by any means, electronic, mechanical, photocopying, recording or otherwise, without the prior written permission of the presenters.

Tash Lewington asserts the moral right to be identified as author of this work.

Presentation by *BookLeaf Publishing*

Web: www.bookleafpub.com

E-mail: info@bookleafpub.com

ISBN: 978-93-95890-29-8

First edition 2022

DEDICATION

Sammy; for the love and supportive messages throughout the process!

Owen; just for being cool and the best and loving me etc.

Laura; for being my ever present source of light without her probably realising, ha.

Charlie; for coming to be by my side whilst I wrote most of this (not that you knew ha) and reminding me of the joys of pushing past the noise and doing the things. And for being a top banter provider for 11 days solid, well done cun.

An Hour Isn't Long Enough.

10am, Saturday morning.

The swirling intricacies bolting inside grey matter, matter too much now. Left unopened under the banner of childhood, unpacking layers of parental dust, tearful remnants of faded pictures sitting betwixt completely blank, erased images,

Stepping slowly into a new view.

We'll Carry On.

In a room bursting with 19,000 and beside a friend from far away,

I declare to the lights,

'I'm just a boy, I'm not a hero.

I

Don't

CARE!!!'

Teen.

Her, in the before times; the tied up shirts and
backwards buttons, floral hair untouchable.

Punctum band t-shirt, slice off sleeves and adjust
the fit to reach around my creativity.

Flash of blue in front, exploring bar and needle
on an afternoon break; curiosity led her to
performing Ionesco whilst cradled in a dream
that she was, at least, a participant of.

I applaud her.

I miss her.

Fuck You Pt I

"I don't know how to help you"

he said.

I knew how to help myself, eventually.

I ran.

You don't keep dancing with the devil and
wonder why you're still in hell.

Sumy.

Dream-following, beautiful entirely and, if I didn't know better, the name referenced next to 'ultimate badass' in the dictionary; snippets of the woman that you are.

I decline referring in tenses past, when death cannot snuff out a fire like yours.

Though past and present collide, the thought sometimes appears

of your last moments.

More importantly,

Thoughts of admiration, warmth and your whiskey chased smile amongst all those who loved you so, wrapped in liquid blue.

The world, and we, were honoured to know you.

Process.

Being the ant, working around the obvious that,
I am here to be considered a pest.

Lock lips and click!

Seething, with no designated space for my low
importance outpour, day in day out as I do the
tired maths; 24 is 3, 1 is asleep, 2 is buzzing
around the bullshit hive, and the third? It is
apparently mine, the same way sand is mine in
hand until

it isn't.

Immortality Currency.

What if.

What if, we were all born with an unknown number of chances, rolls of the proverbial dice; an unknown number of times we can smash our knees in tandem to the surface below, an unknown rhythm in which we should stride or crawl through our hours.

Please Hold.

It sometimes felt like my mind was playing tricks on me. When I remember you, here, physically standing in this room, that you were beside me as I stare through a memory on to the pillow that remains cold beside the one I rest upon. I remember that you held my hand, but I can't remember how it feels.

The innocent thought rushes to the surface first.

'I

Don't

Understand'

Because, you were here. Left your fingerprints and promised you'd come back. (We sit faultless, circumstance bludgeoned us both; I understand, nothing is predicted. All the moving parts glide silently and work beautifully until, one day - everything around them fucking implodes.)

Of course I understand. I understand, the confusion of loving someone who you can't see.

I understand the reason, but not the reality. I understand living around ghosts, now. I understand a heavy numb feeling I carry like a baby in my lower body. I understand the arrogance of time difference. I understand my mind eating itself. I understand thoughts instead of sleep. I understand tears after a group call. I understand the uneasy feeling of experiencing the same scenario twice.

Waltzing the same dance to a mildly different tune.

I understand and long for, when it will change.

Fuck You pt II

This isn't easy

Cringe when I think of consensual.
Why am I crying again because of your
inflictions.
Why did you make this so horrible.

Wonder if my mind has painted it to be worse
than it ever was, but reality bucks and, nope; I
feel the fear rush back in, the jolt to the wall,
tears in eyes and I'm aware I'm in this new room
and I'm trying. I'm trying so fucking hard. You'll
be back tomorrow. Torn between. You ruined it
all. You.

It was YOU. I'M ruined because of YOU.

Travelled lightyears from pain;

Old words die deep.

Fuck You pt III

In a direction towards heaven, dragging my
limbs through hell to reach the top of nothing.

I try.

I keep trying.

I ran to try. Black boxes in a bent room.
Upturned it all to ease the grip of your hands on
my life. 'Perfect' you. It's easy to pretend but
difficult to exist after the storm.

In nothing, something grows.

Young.

You showed me, quickness is key.

Quick to judge, quick to dismiss, quick to doubt.

The lesson of self compassion fell to the side. At twenty four, I remember feeling the first kind words written about me by you. Several sentences, twenty four years late. Words to express how I did not know you felt about me, but I should have been told more often.

Communication, was the sharpened guillotine in my family.

Not A Perfect Science.

The airtime doesn't belong to ALL of the past.

Will making scratches on paper forever, soothe it from my memory?

Let the experiment commence.

(i'll check back in a while, and let me know.)

$142.90

Constant agonising cycle of doubt and doom and disbelief that adulthood is this reliant on all those years before. The thoughts never leave my mind, was I raised cold, or born it.

On the X,
my spine curves.
Pressure, perhaps,
of early years
feeling
frighteningly unloved.

The End of the Show.

They turned all the lights off, as I stand silently proclaiming at my pigeon-nest station.

An empty lift, a red button and a street.

Awaiting (the same) friend from far away, in my new galaxy.

3 Tickets for Brixton Academy.

I have loved you, since I was eighteen; unwavering admiration.

Just a kid,

Black painted 'rebellion', adorned with bows, gestating confidence. Now a wall full of pin holes and a mountain of previously adored armours - living behind the curtain clad door of my teenage years.

Just a kid,

Never severed, scars live on sunk in skin, fondly admired from time to time to time too often.

Just a kid.

Holding my hand, squeezing away the years, as I remember her.

We Own The Night.

Numbed by poison

Walking streets to forget and escape; the boys took turns to hold my hand, since I hadn't found my anchor yet.

Believing in fate

Crying in stalls and screaming at skies until the twilight shifted and there were no more hours left to burn. Even then, excuse after excuse, one more, one more, one more, one more, one, more...

a n y t h i n g

was better than home.

Boy Cinema!

And everything we know now,

Our little life we've crafted out of airplane tickets and tears (from me), normal people things and Halloween decorations, our new apartment and old cold English flat, matching slippers and thousands of messages, walks around cities and evening showers, decaf for you and making breakfast (and dinner) for me, a borrowed pillowcase and a surprise box in my bag, video game co-piloting and long distance love,

Lay then,

On the edge of an un-read message.

Ever On.

Realise the time,

For words before sleep, carry me through to
Sunday.

City lights in statement sky, pushing past to
claim a future.

Even when times are tough and mud is thick;

I promise,

I will care for her.

www.ingramcontent.com/pod-product-compliance
Lightning Source LLC
Chambersburg PA
CBHW061326140726
47998CB00007B/2565

* 9 7 8 9 3 9 5 8 9 0 2 9 8 *